PLANET EARTH

Barbara Taylor

KINGFISHER
NEW YORK

KINGFISHER
LONDON & NEW YORK

Copyright © 2009 by Kingfisher
Published in the United States by Kingfisher,
175 Fifth Ave., New York, NY 10010
Kingfisher is an imprint of Macmillan Children's Books, London.
All rights reserved.

Illustration by Steve Stone (represented by Artist Partners Ltd.)
with additional artwork by Thomas Bayley and Kevin Jones Associates

Consultant: Dr. Rob Francis, King's College London

First published in 2009 by Kingfisher
First published in paperback in 2012 by Kingfisher

Distributed in the U.S. and Canada by Macmillan,
175 Fifth Ave., New York, NY 10010

Library of Congress Cataloging-in-Publication Data
has been applied for.

ISBN: 978-0-7534-6745-9

Kingfisher books are available for special promotions and premiums. For details contact:
Special Markets Department, Macmillan, 175 Fifth Avenue, New York, NY 10010.

For more information, please visit www.kingfisherbooks.com

Printed in China
10 9 8 7 6 5 4 3 2 1

1TR/0911/UTD/WKT/140MA

Note to readers: The website addresses listed in this book are correct at the time of publishing.
However, due to the ever-changing nature of the Internet, website addresses and content can change.
Websites can contain links that are unsuitable for children. The publisher cannot be held responsible for
changes in website addresses or content or for information obtained through third-party websites.
We strongly advise that Internet searches are supervised by an adult.

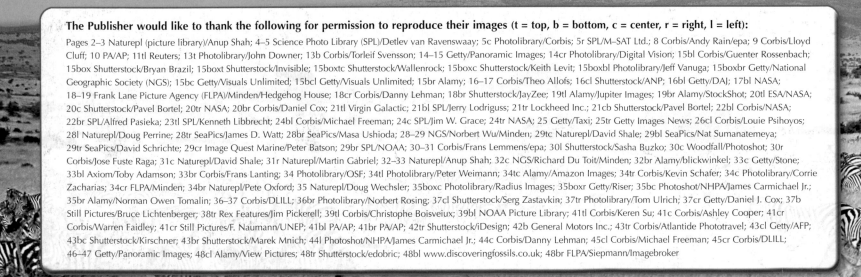

The Publisher would like to thank the following for permission to reproduce their images (t = top, b = bottom, c = center, r = right, l = left):

Pages 2–3 Naturepl (picture library)/Anup Shah; 4–5 Science Photo Library (SPL)/Detlev van Ravensswaay; 5c Photolibrary/Corbis; 5r SPL/M–SAT Ltd.; 8 Corbis/Andy Rain/epa; 9 Corbis/Lloyd Cluff; 10 PA/AP; 11tl Reuters; 13t Photolibrary/John Downer; 13b Corbis/Torleif Svensson; 14–15 Getty/Panoramic Images; 14cr Photolibrary/Digital Vision; 15bl Corbis/Guenter Rossenbach; 15box Shutterstock/Bryan Brazil; 15boxt Shutterstock/Invisible; 15boxtc Shutterstock/Wallenrock; 15boxc Shutterstock/Keith Levit; 15boxbl Photolibrary/Jeff Vanuga; 15boxbr Getty/National Geographic Society (NGS); 15bc Getty/Visuals Unlimited; 15bcl Getty/Visuals Unlimited; 15br Alamy; 16–17 Corbis/Theo Allofs; 16cl Shutterstock/ANP; 16bl Getty/DAJ; 17bl NASA; 18–19 Frank Lane Picture Agency (FLPA)/Minden/Hedgehog House; 18cr Corbis/Danny Lehman; 18br Shutterstock/JayZee; 19tl Alamy/Jupiter Images; 19br Alamy/StockShot; 20tl ESA/NASA; 20c Shutterstock/Pavel Bortel; 20tr NASA; 20br Corbis/Daniel Cox; 21tl Virgin Galactic; 21bl SPL/Jerry Lodriguss; 21tr Lockheed Inc.; 21cb Shutterstock/Pavel Bortel; 22bl Corbis/NASA; 22br SPL/Alfred Pasieka; 23tl SPL/Kenneth Libbrecht; 24bl Corbis/Michael Freeman; 24c SPL/Jim W. Grace; 24tr NASA; 25 Getty/Taxi; 25tr Getty Images News; 26cl Corbis/Louie Psihoyos; 28l Naturepl/Doug Perrine; 28tr SeaPics/James D. Watt; 28br SeaPics/Masa Ushioda; 28–29 NGS/Norbert Wu/Minden; 29tc Naturepl/David Shale; 29bl SeaPics/Nat Sumanatemeya; 29tr SeaPics/David Schrichte; 29cr Image Quest Marine/Peter Batson; 29br SPL/NOAA; 30–31 Corbis/Frans Lemmens/epa; 30l Shutterstock/Sasha Buzko; 30c Woodfall/Photoshot; 30r Corbis/Jose Fuste Raga; 31c Naturepl/David Shale; 31r Naturepl/Martin Gabriel; 32–33 Naturepl/Anup Shah; 32c NGS/Richard Du Toit/Minden; 32br Alamy/blickwinkel; 33c Getty/Stone; 33bl Axiom/Toby Adamson; 33br Corbis/Frans Lanting; 34 Photolibrary/OSF; 34tl Photolibrary/Peter Weimann; 34tc Alamy/Amazon Images; 34tr Corbis/Kevin Schafer; 34c Photolibrary/Corrie Zacharias; 34cr FLPA/Minden; 34br Naturepl/Pete Oxford; 35 Naturepl/Doug Wechsler; 35boxc Photolibrary/Radius Images; 35boxr Getty/Riser; 35bc Photoshot/NHPA/James Carmichael Jr.; 35br Alamy/Norman Owen Tomalin; 36–37 Corbis/DLILL; 36br Photolibrary/Norbert Rosing; 37cl Shutterstock/Serg Zastavkin; 37tr Photolibrary/Tom Ulrich; 37cr Getty/Daniel J. Cox; 37b Still Pictures/Bruce Lichtenberger; 38tr Rex Features/Jim Pickerell; 39tl Corbis/Christophe Boisvieux; 39bl NOAA Picture Library; 41tl Corbis/Keren Su; 41c Corbis/Ashley Cooper; 41cr Corbis/Warren Faidley; 41cr Still Pictures/F. Naumann/UNEP; 41bl PA/AP; 41br PA/AP; 42tr Shutterstock/iDesign; 42b General Motors Inc.; 43tr Corbis/Atlantide Phototravel; 43cl Getty/AFP; 43bc Shutterstock/Kirschner; 43br Shutterstock/Marek Mnich; 44l Photoshot/NHPA/James Carmichael Jr.; 44c Corbis/Danny Lehman; 45cl Corbis/Michael Freeman; 45cr Corbis/DLILL; 46–47 Getty/Panoramic Images; 48cl Alamy/View Pictures; 48tr Shutterstock/edobric; 48bl www.discoveringfossils.co.uk; 48br FLPA/Siepmann/Imagebroker

CONTENTS

EARTH IN SPACE

Earth is a ball of rock spinning in space. It is one of eight planets that orbit (continually travel around) the Sun. The planets probably formed about 4.6 billion years ago from material left over after the Sun was born. Earth is very different from the other planets because it is the only one known to have life and liquid water on its surface. Forces inside planet Earth interact with the air, water, land, and living things on the surface to shape and change the unique world that is our home.

As the third planet from the Sun, Earth is neither too hot nor too cold but just the right temperature for life to survive. Far out in space, the huge planet Jupiter can act as a shield against space rocks that could destroy life on Earth.

Planet water

Almost 70 percent of Earth's surface is covered by water. The four largest areas of water are the Arctic, Atlantic, Indian, and Pacific oceans. There are seven big areas of land (continents): Africa, Antarctica, Asia, Australia, Europe, and North and South America. A blanket of gases called the atmosphere surrounds and protects Earth from the Sun's harmful rays and also from meteors. Swirling white clouds of water form in the atmosphere as the Sun heats Earth's air and water, creating the weather.

> The Moon is about 238,900 mi. (384,400km) from Earth; the Sun is about 93 million mi. (150 million km) away.

"... a sparkling blue and white
jewel, a light, delicate sky-blue sphere
laced with slowly swirling veils of white ...
a small pearl in a thick sea of black mystery.
It takes more than a moment to fully
realize this is Earth ... home."

Edgar Mitchell (born 1930)
*American astronaut,
the sixth person to walk on the Moon*

The Moon

Earth has one moon, which is a ball
of rock that orbits a planet. As well as
orbiting Earth and traveling with the
planet on its long journey around the
Sun, the Moon spins on its own axis.
The Moon pulls at Earth with a force
called gravity. This stops our
planet from wobbling too
much, keeping the climate
stable and allowing
life to develop.

⊖ CHANGING SEASONS

As Earth travels around the Sun once a year,
it tilts at an angle of 23.5°. This tilt makes the
weather in some parts of the world change in
a regular pattern called the seasons. In the
spring and summer seasons, these parts are
tilted toward the Sun and are warmer. In the fall
and winter, they are tilted away and are colder.

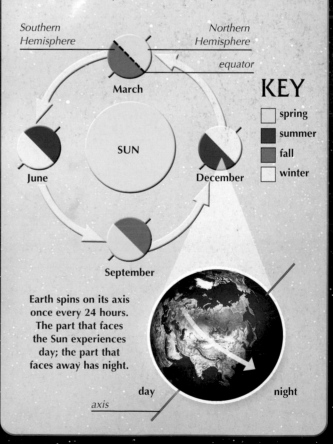

Southern
Hemisphere

Northern
Hemisphere

equator

March

SUN

June

December

September

KEY

spring

summer

fall

winter

**Earth spins on its axis
once every 24 hours.
The part that faces
the Sun experiences
day; the part that
faces away has night.**

day

night

axis

INSIDE EARTH

The surface layer of Earth, the crust, is like the thin skin of an apple. It is divided into about 14 large plates and 38 smaller ones, which fit together like the pieces of a jigsaw puzzle.

The cool blue-and-white face on the outside of Earth hides a boiling hot interior, which may be almost as hot as the surface of the Sun. Even Earth's surface is not quite what it seems. Unlike other planets, its thin surface layer is cracked into gigantic pieces called plates. The heat inside Earth makes these plates slip and slide around, pushing up mountains and volcanoes and causing earthquakes.

PLATES—huge chunks of rock that make up Earth's crust and the top part of the mantle and that move up and down and side to side over time

"Was I to believe him . . . in his intention to penetrate to the center of this massive globe? Had I been listening to the mad speculations of a lunatic, or to the scientific conclusions of a lofty genius?"

Jules Verne (1828–1905)
French author writing in Journey to the Center of the Earth *(1864)*

Growing and shrinking

Over time, Earth's rocky plates, which are 50–250 mi. (80–400km) thick, change in size. They grow if material from inside Earth is added to their edges. They become smaller if they are crushed together or their edges sink back down inside Earth. This means the overall size of the crust stays the same.

PLATES ON THE MOVE

crust

mantle

continental crust

oceanic crust

Hot rocks from inside Earth may burn their way right through the middle of a plate to form islands in the ocean. The Hawaiian Islands were formed in this way.

Deep under the oceans, plates move apart. Hot rocks well up through the gaps and form long ridges of undersea mountains such as those in the middle of the Atlantic and Pacific oceans.

When two plates collide, one plate may be forced beneath the other, causing volcanoes above. The other plate may be pushed upward to form mountains like the Himalayas.

As two plates slide and grind slowly past each other, the rocks may crack apart to form fractures called faults. Earthquakes often happen along faults.

> Earth's plates slide across the surface at about the same speed as your fingernails grow: 0.4–4 in. (1–10cm) per year.

Drilling into Earth

Earth is made up of four main layers. Deep in its center, some 4,000 mi. (6,400km) from the surface, is the inner core, a solid ball most likely made of iron. Although the core is unbelievably hot, at 5,400–9,000°F (3,000–5,000°C), the pressure is so high that it cannot melt. Around this is the slightly cooler outer core, probably made of liquid iron, which creates a magnetic field around Earth. Next comes the mantle, the thickest layer, making up 70–80 percent of the planet. The crust is the final and thinnest layer. It ranges in thickness from 3–6 mi. (5–10km) (oceanic crust) to 9–43 mi. (15–70km) (continental crust).

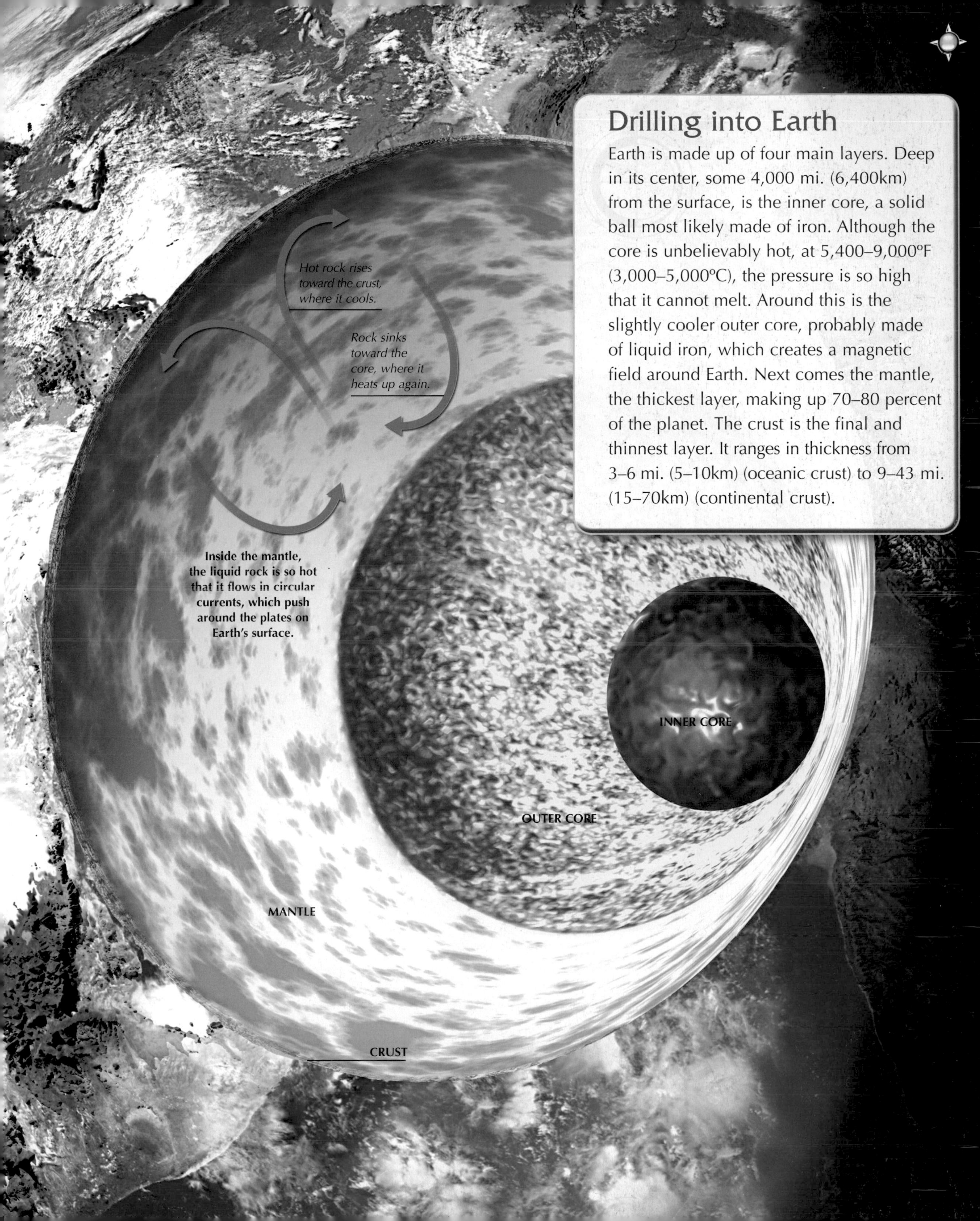

Hot rock rises toward the crust, where it cools.
Rock sinks toward the core, where it heats up again.
Inside the mantle, the liquid rock is so hot that it flows in circular currents, which push around the plates on Earth's surface.
INNER CORE
OUTER CORE
MANTLE
CRUST

www.enchantedlearning.com/subjects/astronomy/planets/earth/contents

Tsunamis

Earthquakes in the ocean can set off enormous waves called tsunamis (*sue-nahm-ees*). These waves travel across the oceans at up to 500 mph (800km/h) and can cross the Pacific Ocean in less than 24 hours. Near the coast, tsunamis can reach heights of 100 ft. (30m). In December 2004, an earthquake in the Indian Ocean triggered a tsunami that devastated many parts of the world.

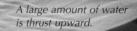

A large amount of water is thrust upward.

FOCUS

OCEANIC CRUST

The thinner, denser plate subducts, or moves beneath, the less dense plate.

A survivor of the 2004 tsunami stands among the rubble where his home once stood in Banda Aceh, Indonesia. The tsunami killed almost 300,000 people.

EARTHQUAKES

Earthquakes happen when a sudden release of energy in Earth's crust causes the ground to shake, sometimes violently. The Richter scale measures the amount of energy released by an earthquake, with catastrophic quakes recording more than 8 on the scale. The biggest earthquakes are caused by plate movements, but earthquakes can also be triggered by volcanic eruptions or artificial explosions. Every year there are probably more than one million earthquakes, although many of these are very small and are not felt by people.

A crack in the crust called a fault forms as blocks of Earth's crust slide past each other during a quake. The focus is the underground starting point of the earthquake. Most damage occurs at the epicenter—the point on the surface directly above the focus.

 > A severe earthquake can be 10,000 times more powerful than the first atomic bomb.

CONTINENTAL CRUST

When one plate is forced beneath another, earthquakes can occur in the crust above.
If such an earthquake occurs in the ocean, a tsunami forms.

The thicker, less dense plate crumples upward as it collides with the other plate.

Moving and shaking

During an earthquake, Earth's rocks crack and shudder, causing shock waves, or seismic waves, that spread from the place where the quake started underground. This location is called the focus of the earthquake. The waves travel inside Earth and along its surface. Their speed depends on the depth of the focus and the strength of the rocks through which they move. Waves from very large earthquakes can cause the whole planet to ring like a tuning fork for an entire day.

Earthquakes often occur along faults, such as the San Andreas Fault (right) in California. Faults are lines of weakness in Earth's crust.

fault

Shock waves called seismic waves ripple out from the focus.

EPICENTER

FOCUS

The focus of deep earthquakes may occur more than 430 mi. (700km) below Earth's surface.

VOLCANOES

Volcanoes are openings on Earth's surface through which hot molten rock (magma), ash, and gas can escape. They release pressure that builds up under the ground and help cool Earth's fiery core. Most of Earth's volcanoes occur along plate edges, where the crust is weakest and the magma can easily burst through. There are more than 500 active volcanoes in the world, and one in ten people live in areas threatened by volcanic eruptions.

MAGMA—very hot molten (liquid) rock from Earth's crust and mantle deep underground

In 1997, Plymouth, on the Caribbean island of Montserrat, was buried under more than 39 ft. (12m) of mud and ash after a nearby volcano erupted. The town was abandoned permanently.

Fire mountain

When magma pours out of a volcano and onto Earth's surface, it is called lava. This volcano (right) has formed a mountain made of layers of ash and lava, which have cooled down and turned into hard rock. The shape of a volcano depends on the type of lava. Thick and sticky lava does not flow far before it becomes solid, so it forms dome-shaped volcanoes. Thin and runny lava spreads out across wider areas to form low, flat shapes called shield volcanoes.

> Red hot lava, which can reach more than 1,800°F (1,000°C), flows out of a volcano at up to 590 ft. (180m)/s.

In May 2008, Chile's Chaitén volcano erupted after 9,000 years, throwing clouds of ash more than 10 mi. (16km) into the sky and depositing ash hundreds of miles away in Argentina.

KEY

1. laccolith—a chamber of magma that forces the rock above it into a dome shape

2. magma chamber—an underground pool of molten (liquid) rock

3. main vent—the passage through which magma escapes to the surface

4. geyser—a fountain of boiling hot water and steam, heated by hot volcanic rock

5. hot spring—water, also heated under the ground, that bubbles to the surface and colors the ground with its minerals

6. fissure vent—a long, thin crack, sometimes several miles in length, through which lava erupts

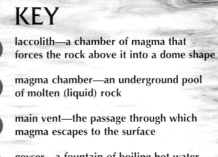

Robots collect samples of gas and rock from volcanic areas that are too dangerous for people to reach.

www.fema.gov/kids/volcano.htm

MOUNTAINS

RANGE—a group or chain of mountains

About one-fifth of Earth's surface is made up of mountains. These steep-sided areas, usually more than 3,300 ft. (1,000m) tall, dominate the landscape around them. The world's biggest mountain ranges include the Alps of Europe, the Himalayas of Asia, the Rocky Mountains of North America, and the Andes of South America. There are even huge mountains under the sea.

Fold mountains

These mountains form when two of Earth's plates crash into each other, pushing up the layers of rock between them into gigantic bends called folds. The Himalayas are still being pushed upward by about 2 in (6cm) every year.

Fault-block mountains

Block mountains form when pressure beneath Earth's crust pushes huge chunks of land upward between two faults, or cracks, in the crust. Like most block mountains, Table Mountain in South Africa has a flat top, not the jagged peaks of fold mountains.

BLOCK MOVES UP

BLOCK MOVES DOWN

fault line

> Volcanic mountain Mauna Kea, Hawaii, is 33,480 ft. (10,205m) tall (taller than Everest), but most of it lies under the ocean.

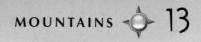

Bar-headed geese fly over the Himalayas from feeding grounds in India to nesting sites in Tibet. They can extract oxygen from the very thin mountain air.

Dome mountains

Sometimes magma pushes up the crust without folding or faulting it, or breaking through to the surface. When this occurs, the land bulges upward into a rounded shape called a dome mountain.

LACCOLITH

MAGMA CHAMBER

PLATES MOVING TOGETHER

Volcanic mountains

Volcanic mountains, such as Mount Kilimanjaro in East Africa, form when magma from beneath the crust escapes onto the surface and builds up, layer upon layer, into a huge mound of rock.

Making mountains

Mountains are pushed upward by the movements of Earth's plates or by magma from deep inside the mantle forcing its way through the crust. Mountains are evidence of forces inside our planet that are strong enough to move enormous areas of rock over millions of years. Some mountains are still growing taller, while others are being worn away and will one day be flat land again.

Mount Kilimanjaro, an extinct volcano, is 19,340 ft. (5,895m) tall and is the highest mountain in Africa. It is located in Tanzania, about 200 mi. (322km) south of the equator.

"Mountains are the beginning and the end of all natural scenery."

John Ruskin (1819–1900)
British art critic and author

Standing stones

In Nambung National Park, Western Australia, stand thousands of spectacular limestone pillars, some of them 13 ft. (4m) tall. The pillars are all that remain of a thick layer of hard limestone rock that formed under sand dunes. Over thousands of years, the wind blew away the loose sand to reveal the columns of rock.

ROCKS AND MINERALS

Rocks are the solid materials that make up Earth's crust. They are full of clues about our planet's past because their characteristics depend on how and where they were formed. All rocks are made of mixtures of natural chemicals, called minerals, that usually form crystals and are stuck together in solid chunks. There are three main types of rocks: igneous, sedimentary, and metamorphic.

Igneous rocks

These rocks are formed when magma escapes through cracks in the crust and then cools and hardens on the surface. The Giant's Causeway in Ireland (above) was created about 60 million years ago by volcanoes that erupted, leaving a lava pond. The 40,000 columns formed as the lava cooled, shrank, and cracked. Most of the columns are six-sided.

> Coal is made from dead swamp plants pressed tightly together over millions of years.

Sedimentary rocks

These rocks are made from sediments—small grains of sand, mud, and other debris removed from rocks by wind and water. They are also made from the remains of plants and animals. The sediments collect in layers on the bottom of oceans, lakes, and rivers. Eventually, the weight of all the layers squeezes out the water, pressing the sediments into solid rock such as sandstone, limestone, or chalk.

www.minsocam.org/MSA/k12/rkcycle/rkcycleindex.html

⊖ THE ROCK CYCLE

Rocks are continually forming, being destroyed and remade in a recycling process called the rock cycle. New rocks form when volcanoes erupt, but old rocks are eroded, or worn away, by wind and water. Old rocks can be changed into new ones by pressure, heat, and forces inside Earth.

IGNEOUS ROCK

weathering, erosion

cooling, solidifying

melting

heat, pressure

sediments

compacting

weathering, erosion

melting

magma

melting

weathering, erosion

SEDIMENTARY ROCK

heat, pressure

METAMORPHIC ROCK

Metamorphic rocks

When igneous or sedimentary rocks are baked by red hot magma or squeezed by powerful plate movements, metamorphic rock is created. The sedimentary rock limestone changes with heat and pressure into the metamorphic rock marble (below).

Minerals

Minerals are basic natural substances, usually made of two or more chemical elements such as oxygen, silicon, calcium, iron, or sodium. Minerals form when the elements in a gas or a liquid change into solid shapes with flat sides and angled edges called crystals.

Quartz, a very common mineral, is a major ingredient of most igneous and metamorphic rocks.

Hematite is made of iron and oxygen and has been mined as a source of iron since ancient times.

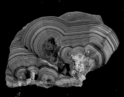

Malachite often has distinctive green bands. The bright green tarnish on copper is malachite.

RIVERS AND COASTS

The water in rivers and oceans is a powerful force that shapes the surface of planet Earth. It can break up rocks and soil, carrying them away to carve valleys, caves, bays, and headlands. And it can deposit the rocks and soil as sediment to form floodplains, deltas, beaches, and salt marshes. The gradual breaking down of rocks by the weather, plants, and chemicals is called weathering. The carrying away of this rocky material by wind, water, and moving rivers of ice (glaciers) is called erosion.

⬤ SHAPING THE COAST

As waves crash against the shore, throwing sand and pebbles at soft rock, bays are carved into the coastline. Harder rock survives to stick out as headlands. If waves hollow out caves on either side of a headland, a rock arch forms. And if the top of the arch collapses, a tall pillar called a stack is left.

salt marsh—where plants grow in protected, shallow, water

dunes

headland

bay

cave

arch

stack

spit—ridge formed by longshore drift moving material out to sea

lagoon—coastal lake cut off from the ocean by a sandbar

estuary— wide mouth of a river on the coast

arrows show longshore drift sideways movement of beach material if waves strike coast at an angle

Mangroves

In the Everglades National Park, Florida, mangroves help protect the coast from strong waves and storms. Their tangled, stiltlike roots trap mud, helping build up new land. The roots also anchor the muddy soil during hurricanes.

Nile River's delta

In 1971, a dam was built across the Nile River near the city of Aswan. The dam generated electricity and irrigated crops, but it also stopped the river from carrying sediments down to the delta. Now the outer edges of the delta are being worn away by the sea and the soil is becoming more salty.

DELTA—a build-up of sediments deposited by a river when its current slows as it meets the ocean

> Tides are caused by the pull of gravity from the Moon and the Sun, whereas waves are driven by the wind.

Water highways

As a river winds back and forth across the land like a natural highway carrying water and sediments instead of cars, it can carve sharp bends called meanders. The precise shape and path of the river and its side channels depend on the type of soil and rock around them as well as on the slope of the land.

This river in Kimberley, Western Australia, meanders across a floodplain.

This false-color satellite image shows the fan-shaped delta of the Nile River in Egypt.

"Deeply regret [to] advise you: Titanic sank this morning after collision with iceberg, resulting in serious loss of life. Full particulars later."

Joseph Bruce Ismay (1862–1937)
Survivor of the sinking of the RMS Titanic sending a message to New York City after the 1912 disaster

Rivers of ice

A glacier forms when snow piles up in a mountain valley and, at its base, becomes squeezed into ice—like pressing together soft snow to make an icy snowball. The glacier is pulled downhill by gravity, causing deep cracks on its surface. Eventually, the glacier reaches warmer places and slowly melts, depositing the rocks and soil that it has been carrying.

Sawyer Glacier, Alaska

ICE SHEETS AND GLACIERS

Earth's water is strange stuff. As well as existing in liquid form, it also turns into a solid called ice when the temperature drops below freezing. The largest continuous area of ice in the world is the vast ice sheet covering the continent of Antarctica. The North Pole is surrounded by a huge frozen ocean, the Arctic Ocean, and down from the tops of Earth's cold mountains, rivers of ice called glaciers slowly flow. As the glaciers move along, they dig up rocks and carry them down mountains, carving valleys into deep "U" shapes.

A group of visitors to Antarctica views a huge overturned iceberg close to Enterprise Island.

> Ice covers about 10 percent of Earth's land and about 12 percent of its oceans.

Clues in the rock

As a glacier moves along, pieces of rock trapped in the ice grind and scrape away at the ground like sandpaper, leaving scars on the landscape. These marks indicate the size and flow direction of glaciers that passed over the rock long ago. Thicker glaciers press down harder and carve out deeper grooves than thinner glaciers.

⊖ STUDYING GLACIERS

A scientist who studies glaciers, and ice in general, is called a glaciologist. Like frozen chunks of history, glaciers can tell scientists about Earth's climate in the past. Their size, shape, and speed can also teach scientists about today's climate. About 75 percent of Earth's fresh water is locked away in glaciers and ice sheets.

Icebergs

In the cold polar regions at the top and bottom of the world, huge chunks of ice break off glaciers and ice sheets and float away into the oceans as icebergs. Ice floats on water, but only just, so about 90 percent of an iceberg is hidden under the water. The hidden part of the iceberg is very dangerous to ships in polar waters.

This glaciologist is using crampons and ice axes to haul himself up a glacier to examine its structure.

EARTH'S BLANKET

Wrapped around Earth is a thin blanket of gases called the atmosphere, and life on Earth could not exist without it. As well as providing air to keep animals and plants alive, the atmosphere stops Earth from getting too hot or too cold and protects the planet from the Sun's harmful rays. It is made of a mixture of gases, mostly nitrogen (from volcanoes) and oxygen (from plants).

EXOSPHERE

Air is constantly "exiting" into space, which is why this layer is called the exosphere. The Hubble Space Telescope and some satellites are here, although many satellites reach heights of 22,200 mi. (35,800km).

280 mi. (450km) above Earth

The space shuttle would enter orbit at about 185 mi. (300km).

Ocean satellite

Jason 2, an oceanography satellite, circles 830 mi. (1,336km) above Earth. It monitors sea levels and the distribution of heat in the oceans. This enables us to make more accurate weather forecasts, predict climate change, and examine links between the oceans and atmosphere.

From Earth to space

Earth's atmosphere is about 620 mi. (1,000km) thick. It is divided into five layers of differing temperatures—but each layer fades into the next one with no distinct dividing lines. The air gets thinner higher up in the atmosphere, which is why people usually take oxygen supplies with them when climbing mountains.

From orbit, Earth's fragile atmosphere looks like a thin blue line around the planet. Resting on top of the atmosphere is red light from the setting Sun.

THERMOSPHERE

This is the hottest layer of the atmosphere, reaching temperatures as high as 3,600°F (2,000°C) at the top. The International Space Station and some satellites orbit (move around) Earth in this layer.

Light show

Spectacular colored light displays in the night skies of polar regions are called auroras, or the northern and southern lights. Auroras are caused by radiation from the Sun hitting the outer layers of Earth's atmosphere, creating electric currents that make the gases glow.

Shooting stars

Shooting stars, or meteor showers, blazing a trail across the night sky are caused by debris from a comet entering Earth's atmosphere at very high speed. The debris rapidly burns up, leaving jets of bright light shooting across the sky. Most meteor showers produce only a few meteors per hour.

> OXYGEN—*a gas that is produced by plants and that all living things need to survive*

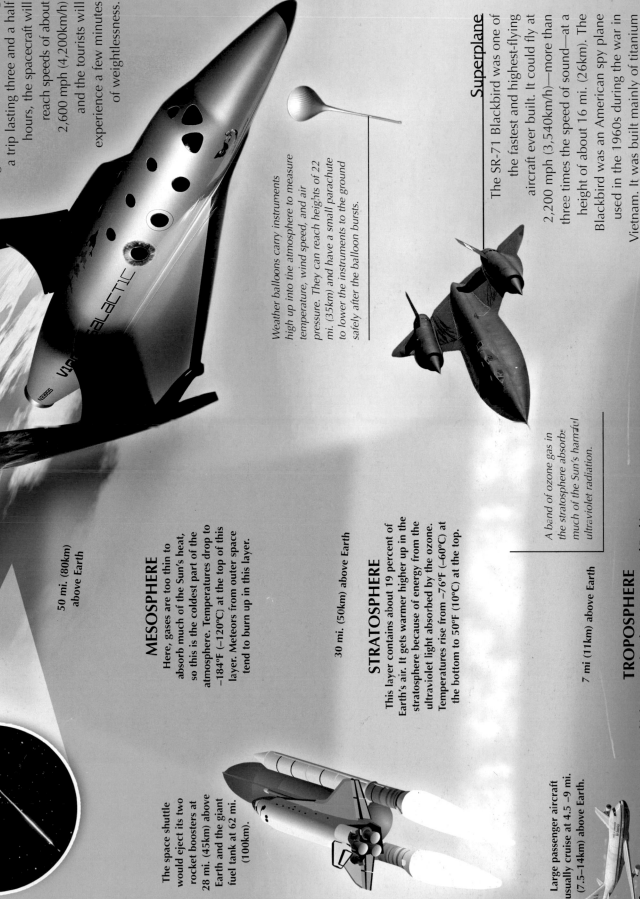

Space tourists

SpaceShipTwo is a small spacecraft designed to carry six space tourists into the thermosphere up to a height of 68 mi. (110km). During a trip lasting three and a half hours, the spacecraft will reach speeds of about 2,600 mph (4,200km/h) and the tourists will experience a few minutes of weightlessness.

Weather balloons carry instruments high up into the atmosphere to measure temperature, wind speed, and air pressure. They can reach heights of 22 mi. (35km) and have a small parachute to lower the instruments to the ground safely after the balloon bursts.

Superplane

The SR-71 Blackbird was one of the fastest and highest-flying aircraft ever built. It could fly at 2,200 mph (3,540km/h)—more than three times the speed of sound—at a height of about 16 mi. (26km). The Blackbird was an American spy plane used in the 1960s during the war in Vietnam. It was built mainly of titanium to withstand the heat generated by friction during supersonic flight.

50 mi. (80km) above Earth

MESOSPHERE

Here, gases are too thin to absorb much of the Sun's heat, so this is the coldest part of the atmosphere. Temperatures drop to −184°F (−120°C) at the top of this layer. Meteors from outer space tend to burn up in this layer.

30 mi. (50km) above Earth

STRATOSPHERE

This layer contains about 19 percent of Earth's air. It gets warmer higher up in the stratosphere because of energy from the ultraviolet light absorbed by the ozone. Temperatures rise from −76°F (−60°C) at the bottom to 50°F (10°C) at the top.

A band of ozone gas in the stratosphere absorbs much of the Sun's harmful ultraviolet radiation.

7 mi. (11km) above Earth

TROPOSPHERE

This layer contains about 80 percent of Earth's air. All living things, as well as weather conditions, are concentrated in this layer.

The space shuttle would eject its two rocket boosters at 28 mi. (45km) above Earth and the giant fuel tank at 62 mi. (100km).

Large passenger aircraft usually cruise at 4.5 –9 mi. (7.5–14km) above Earth.

❯ The atmosphere is made up of about 76 percent nitrogen, 21 percent oxygen, and three percent other gases such as carbon dioxide.

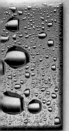

WEATHER AND WATER

The Sun's heat stirs up Earth's atmosphere, making air and water move from place to place. This creates clouds, wind, and all sorts of weather. The weather on Earth changes all the time, mostly because of all the water on the planet's surface. The world's water is never used up. It just moves from the land or the oceans up into the sky and back down again in a never-ending loop called the water cycle.

WATER CYCLE—the continuous movement of water—as liquid, solid (ice), and vapor—on, above, and below Earth's surface

Condensation
As the air full of water vapor rises, it cools down because temperatures decrease higher up. Cool air cannot hold as much water vapor as warm air can, so some of the vapor turns back into droplets of water. This process of a gas changing into a liquid when it cools is called condensation. The droplets of condensed water gather to form clouds.

Cumulus clouds look like fluffy cotton.

satellite photograph of the Northern Hemisphere's jet stream carrying clouds over Egypt and the Red Sea

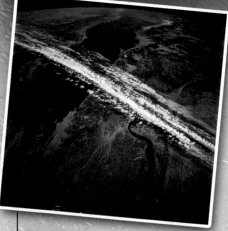

Icy cirrus clouds mark the position of a strong wind called the jet stream, which blows more than 120 mph (200km/h) about 6 mi. (10km) above Earth. There are two jet streams—one in each hemisphere—and they move large masses of air. This has a major impact on the world's weather.

Evaporation
When liquid water is heated, it turns into an invisible gas called water vapor and disappears into the air. This process of a liquid changing into a gas when it is heated is called evaporation. The warm air containing the evaporated water is less dense, and therefore lighter, than the liquid water, so it rises up into the sky.

When water vapor in the air condenses onto cold glass, drops of water form. A similar process occurs inside clouds.

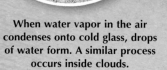

Each raindrop is made up of a million cloud droplets.

In very cold air, water droplets freeze into tiny ice crystals, which stick together to make snowflakes.

Precipitation

Clouds are made up of masses of tiny water droplets hanging in the sky. When the droplets bump into one another, they form large drops of water that are too heavy to stay in the cloud. This causes precipitation—water falling as rain, snow, or hail.

Water vapor and clouds are blown by the wind, so rain often falls a long distance from where the water first evaporated.

http://kids.earth.nasa.gov/droplet.html

Transpiration is the process by which water evaporates from plants, mostly through their leaves.

Infiltration is the process of water seeping down through rocks and soil.

The "ground water" reaches a layer that won't absorb it and moves downhill to the sea.

The surface of the ground water is the water table.

The water cycle

When the Sun heats the water in oceans, on land, or in living things, the water evaporates into the air and rises up into the sky. There, it cools down and condenses to form clouds, which release the water as rain, snow, or hail. When the Sun heats the water on the surface, the cycle starts all over again.

STORMY WEATHER

Every so often, the atmosphere is disturbed by violent storms caused by powerful winds and towering, swirling clouds. This extreme weather brings heavy rain, blizzards, floods, thunder and lightning, and winds that destroy everything in their path. In hot, tropical areas, storms happen because of the heat and moisture in the air. In cooler areas, storms usually occur where enormous areas of warm and cold air meet along weather fronts. Storms carry heat away from the tropics, helping even out global temperatures.

⊖ HURRICANES

Hurricanes (also called typhoons or cyclones) form over warm oceans. The Sun heats moisture in the air, causing it to rise and condense into storm clouds that swirl around—because the planet is spinning around. Strong winds circle upward around a calm area called the eye. When a hurricane moves over land, its supply of moisture (and source of energy) is cut off and it begins to fade.

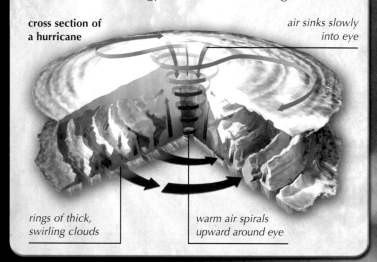

cross section of a hurricane

air sinks slowly into eye

rings of thick, swirling clouds

warm air spirals upward around eye

Blizzards

Snowstorms with low temperatures, strong winds, and a heavy fall of fine, powdery snow are called blizzards. The snowflakes zoom rapidly through the air, swirling around and making it difficult to see far ahead. The wind may blow the snow into mounds called drifts.

Sandstorms

Powerful winds blowing down from storm clouds have taken only a few minutes to push up this massive wall of sand and dust. It is moving rapidly toward a livestock market in Sudan, Africa. A sandstorm with a speeding sand wall like this is called a haboob.

As many as 50,000 storms happen every day around the world. In the United States, there are about 1,000 tornadoes every year.

www.skydiary.com/kids

This home, in Iowa, was destroyed by a tornado that ripped through the Midwestern states in May 2008.

Twisters

A twister, or tornado, is a spinning funnel of wind that extends from a huge whirling storm cloud called a supercell. Winds at different levels in the atmosphere come from different directions, pushing around the storm cloud like a spinning top. Tornadoes, which are usually narrow, suck up everything like a giant vacuum cleaner. Winds can reach up to 250 mph (400km/h).

"We're not on the ground, Toto! . . .
We must be up inside the [tornado]!"

Dorothy talks to her dog, Toto
From the 1939 movie The Wizard of Oz

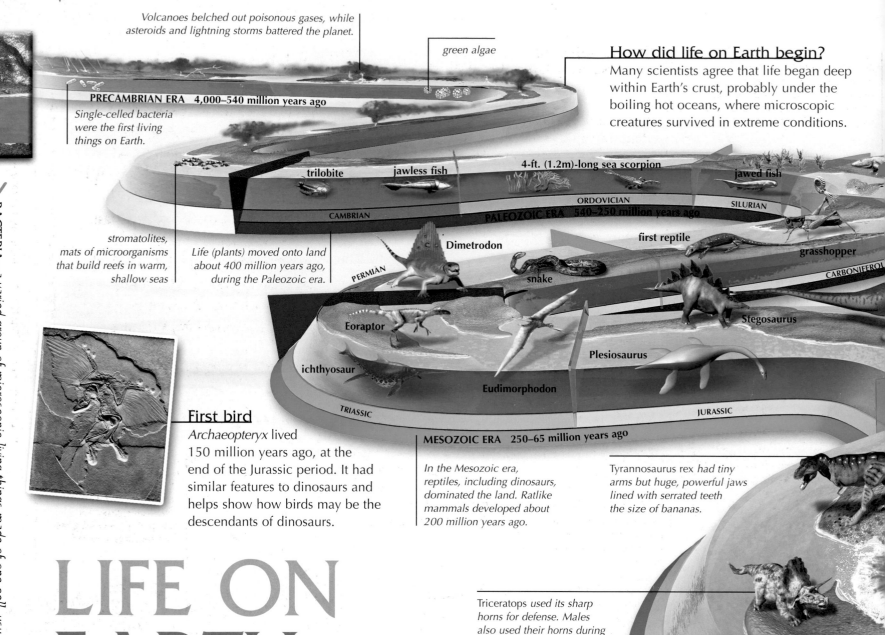

Volcanoes belched out poisonous gases, while asteroids and lightning storms battered the planet.

green algae

How did life on Earth begin?
Many scientists agree that life began deep within Earth's crust, probably under the boiling hot oceans, where microscopic creatures survived in extreme conditions.

PRECAMBRIAN ERA   4,000–540 million years ago

Single-celled bacteria were the first living things on Earth.

stromatolites, mats of microorganisms that build reefs in warm, shallow seas

trilobite

jawless fish

4-ft. (1.2m)-long sea scorpion

jawed fish

ORDOVICIAN

SILURIAN

CAMBRIAN

PALEOZOIC ERA   540–250 million years ago

Life (plants) moved onto land about 400 million years ago, during the Paleozoic era.

Dimetrodon

first reptile

grasshopper

PERMIAN

snake

CARBONIFEROU

Eoraptor

Stegosaurus

ichthyosaur

Plesiosaurus

Eudimorphodon

TRIASSIC

JURASSIC

First bird
Archaeopteryx lived 150 million years ago, at the end of the Jurassic period. It had similar features to dinosaurs and helps show how birds may be the descendants of dinosaurs.

MESOZOIC ERA   250–65 million years ago

In the Mesozoic era, reptiles, including dinosaurs, dominated the land. Ratlike mammals developed about 200 million years ago.

Tyrannosaurus rex had tiny arms but huge, powerful jaws lined with serrated teeth the size of bananas.

LIFE ON EARTH

Triceratops used its sharp horns for defense. Males also used their horns during wrestling matches to decide which individual would dominate the herd.

CRETACEOUS

Life began on Earth at least 3.8 billion years ago. For about two billion years, there were only microscopic bacteria-like creatures, but 600 million years ago, life took off in the oceans. Over millions of years, creatures moved onto land, developing and changing until the whole planet was covered with living things, including humans.

The dinosaurs
Dinosaurs ruled the world for more than 150 million years, from the Triassic to the Cretaceous periods. There were at least 1,000 different kinds, from the giant sauropods and terrifying tyrannosaurs to dinosaurs with gigantic horns or bills like ducks. There were 30 times more plant eaters than meat eaters.

 > Earth's first, microscopic life forms may have come from space with asteroids or comets, possibly from Mars.

The first amphibians evolved from fish. They could live both in the sea—with the ammonites, stingrays, and sharks—and on land. They developed ways to extract oxygen from air instead of water.

DEVONIAN

The biggest dinosaurs were the plant-eating sauropods such as Diplodocus.

Natural selection

Over time, living things adapt physically to their environment. Those species best suited to it survive to pass on their genetic characteristics to the next generation, while other species die out. This "natural selection" or "survival of the fittest" was first suggested by Charles Darwin and Alfred Russel Wallace in the 1800s.

berry feeding   seed feeding   cactus feeding

Darwin noted that finches on the Galápagos Islands had evolved different beaks for eating different foods.

The dinosaurs were wiped out at the end of the Cretaceous period, when a comet is thought to have struck Earth.

Spinosaurus

A history of life

Scientists have pieced together the development of life on Earth by dating rocks and studying the fossilized remains of creatures. Only a tiny fraction of living things become fossils, so there are many gaps in our knowledge of the past. Fossil evidence shows that fish developed into amphibians, which gave rise to the first true land animals, reptiles. Birds and mammals evolved from reptiles.

The rise of humankind

Fossils of our human ancestors show that skull size gradually increased to make room for a larger brain. Hipbones also changed to allow walking on two legs, freeing the hands to use tools. Humans are thought to have evolved in Africa.

During the Cenozoic era, mammals developed into a large variety of forms. In the Neogene period, climates cooled and grasslands spread. Apes, including our own ancestors, evolved.

During Earth's history, there have been several glacial periods, when ice sheets covered large parts of the planet.

penguin

Brontotherium

Australopithecus

toad

Homo sapiens

kangaroo

pelican

Turtles have lived for more than 220 million years, since the earliest days of the dinosaurs.

woolly mammoth

human settlements

Prosqualodon

killer whale

PALEOGENE

NEOGENE

QUATERNARY

CENOZOIC ERA   65 million years ago–present day

OCEANS

The oceans cover more than 70 percent of the planet and include the Pacific, Atlantic, Indian, Antarctic, and Arctic oceans as well as smaller seas. Under the oceans lies a dramatic landscape of huge mountain ranges, deep valleys, and vast plains. Oceans have a huge impact on the weather, absorbing heat and spreading it around the world with their ocean currents.

Bottlenosed dolphins use their powerful tails to push themselves up out of the ocean.

The sunlit zone

This zone receives the most light and heat. It extends from the surface down to about 330–500 ft. (100–150m). This is the only zone in which plants can grow. Predators such as dolphins, sharks, and tuna hunt in the sunlit zone.

Whale sharks, the biggest fish in the world, feed only on tiny drifting plants and animals called plankton.

The twilight zone

It is quite light in the upper part of the twilight zone during the day, but the lower part—some 3,300 ft. (1,000m) beneath the surface—is always dark. The Sun's rays cannot reach this deep into the ocean, and many animals produce their own light for camouflage or to find food or mates. Animals feed on one another or on animal and plant remains that

The green sea turtle has powerful flippers to "fly" underwater. It spends most of its life in oceans, but females lay their eggs on beaches.

The building blocks of coral reefs are the skeletons of tiny anemone-like animals called polyps. Living polyps colonize the skeletons. The polyps can live only in clean, warm, salty water less than 100 ft. (30m) deep as the algae living in them need sunlight to make food.

> OCEAN CURRENT—a "river" of water flowing through an ocean, both near the surface and much deeper

Zones of life

There is life at all levels in the oceans, from the sunlit surface to the deep darkness of the ocean floor. In each zone, creatures are specially adapted to the different conditions of temperature, light, and salinity (the saltiness of the water).

Most sea creatures live in the sunlit zone, but some do move from one zone to another.

Anglerfish have a built-in "fishing rod" with a glowing tip to lure prey toward them.

With earlike fins on top of its body, the dumbo octopus is named after Walt Disney's flying elephant. It lives at depths of 9,800–13,100 ft. (3,000–4,000m), hovering above the sea floor to hunt worms, shellfish and other prey.

The giant isopod looks a lot like its pill bug relative—but it is the size of a brick! It lives in the Antarctic Ocean and scavenges for scraps of food on the seabed.

The weedy sea dragon, a type of sea horse, is well camouflaged by fleshy flaps that resemble seaweed.

The dark zone

The vast, completely dark zone of the deep ocean stretches down to 19,700 ft. (6,000m) or more. Sea cucumbers dominate the ocean floor, sucking food scraps from the surface of the mud. Many deep-sea animals, such as sponges, sea anemones, and tubeworms, sit and wait for food to fall down on them from the zones above.

Superhot water gushes out of vents in black plumes. Bacteria get their energy from the chemicals in these "black smokers" and provide food for animals such as giant tubeworms. Vent bacteria can withstand higher temperatures than any other living thing.

❯ On the ocean floor, a Styrofoam cup shrinks to about the size of a thimble because of the crushing pressure.

DESERTS

The driest places on the planet (usually with less than 10 in., or 25cm, of rain per year), deserts cover almost one-third of Earth's land surface. During the day, they are baking hot, but at night, temperatures can plummet to below freezing because there are few clouds or plants to hold heat near the ground. High winds, bare rocks, shifting sand dunes, and rare floods make deserts hostile environments for living things.

This giant saguaro cactus, in the Sonoran Desert, Arizona, grew its arms when it was 75 years old—it may live for more than 200 years. When it rains, the pleats in its stem expand like an accordian, allowing the cactus to take in as much water as possible.

Oases

In a few places in a desert, water comes to the surface to form a moist area called an oasis. The water often comes from rain that falls on mountains far away and travels underground through rocks that hold water. A pool of water collects in a hollow that dips below the top of the water table.

Crescent Lake is a natural oasis in the Gobi Desert in China. However, artificial oases can be created by digging wells in places where the water table is close to the surface.

Plant life

Plants have to be very tough to survive in deserts because they can't hide from the sun as animals can. They store water in their stems and leaves and soak up moisture with wide-spreading roots that tap into water deep underground. Some plants survive when their seeds are buried in the desert soil. The seeds lie in wait for a rare rainstorm to help them sprout.

> There is enough water in a giant saguaro cactus to fill 1,000 bathtubs!

Desert dunes

In some deserts, such as the Sahara, the wind blows sand into vast areas called sand seas or ergs. Within the ergs, huge piles of sand, or dunes, move with the wind, changing shape like waves on the sea. The shape of a dune depends on the amount of sand as well as the wind speed and direction. Crescent-shaped barchan dunes form where the wind blows from the same direction. Seif dunes are steep ridges of sand.

"One day, we had to advance in the teeth of the [sand]storm . . . To stop means to be drowned by the sand. The camels instinctively know this and continue to advance in spite of the tormenting blast."

Ahmed Hassanein (1889–1946)
Egyptian politician and explorer writing about his travels in the Libyan Desert

www.mbgnet.net/sets/desert/

Sand dunes in the Sahara Desert, the biggest desert in the world, cover an area almost as big as the United States.

⊖ DESERT ANIMALS

Most desert animals survive with very little water, often getting all the water they need from their food. Kangaroo rats don't drink at all. They hide from the heat of the day in burrows, emerging in the cool of the night to search for food. Camels store fat in their humps and break this down to provide food and water when needed. A camel has wide feet to keep it from sinking into the sand and long eyelashes to keep sand out of its eyes.

The scaly skin of reptiles, such as this chameleon (right), prevents water loss. Reptiles can survive higher temperatures than birds or mammals.

The big ears of the sand fox work like radiators to transfer heat into the air to cool the animal.

PREDATOR—an animal that hunts other animals for food

Tropical grasslands

One of the two main types of grassland is the tropical savanna of Africa, India, and Australia. Some of the largest animals on the planet—elephants and giraffes—live on the African savanna. These warm grasslands have wet and dry seasons, and animals move around following the rains, which help fresh grass grow.

Land of the llama

Grasslands grow on flat plains high up in the Andes Mountains of South America. They are grazed by llamas, which were tamed by the Inca some 6,000 years ago. They are still used for carrying supplies today, as well as for their wool and meat.

GRASSLANDS

Covering about one-fourth of the planet, grasslands grow in between regions of wet forests and dry deserts. Few trees survive in grasslands because either the weather is too dry or the soil is too poor. In some areas, grazing animals or fires keep young trees from growing, allowing grasslands to spread. Grasslands are home to large grass-eating animals (grazers), such as antelope, as well as the predators that feed on them and the scavengers that clean up their leftovers. Small animals burrow beneath grasslands to hide from predators.

> Termite nests can contain up to 20 million individual termites and can be as tall as a giraffe.

⊖ COOL GRASSLANDS

Cooler, temperate grasslands are found in Asia (steppes), South America (pampas), and North America (prairies). Temperate grasslands usually develop in the middle of continents or in the rain shadows of high mountains where rainfall is low. People use temperate grasslands to graze animals or to grow crops such as wheat and corn.

This farmer is using camels to cut grass for making hay on the steppes of Mongolia.

Zebras live in large herds on the African grasslands. These wild, striped horses bite off the tough tops of grasses, encouraging new shoots to grow from the bases of the plants.

Blazing grasslands

Fires are often started by lightning storms at the end of the dry season. Dry grasses catch on fire easily and burn quickly. Fires destroy most trees and other large, slow-growing plants, but grasses soon sprout back. People sometimes start fires to encourage grasses to grow and to create more land for crops or grazing cattle.

Termite mounds on the African savanna provide food for bat-eared foxes. The foxes use their keen hearing to find the termites before licking them up.

Termite territory

Insects called termites construct huge nests on tropical grasslands. They build them with soil, saliva, and droppings, which set to form a rock-hard shelter from the heat. Millions of termites live inside, eating decaying material or using it as compost to grow fungi for food.

bat-eared foxes

FORESTS

Thousands of years ago, forests covered about half of planet Earth's land, but today they cover less than one-third. Forests are cut down for their wood and other natural resources and to make space for farms and towns. Yet forests provide food, water, and shelter for a huge variety of wildlife. They cool the planet by giving shade, recycle water through their leaves, and regulate the amount of oxygen and carbon dioxide in the atmosphere. Without forests, the planet would be a much more hostile environment for life.

Rainforest roof

Most of the wildlife in a rainforest lives in the roof of the forest, called the canopy, which is about 130 ft. (40m) above the ground. This layer receives the most rain and sun, which means it has the most leaves, flowers, and fruit for animals such as monkeys and birds to eat.

A few very tall trees peek out from the canopy to form the "emergent layer."

Rainforests

These tropical forests grow in a band around the equator, where the weather is hot and wet all year long. They cover only six percent of Earth's land surface, but more than half of the world's different species of living things live there. There are four main areas of rainforest: in Central and South America, in Africa, in Southeast Asia, and in Australasia.

> NATURAL RESOURCE—*a naturally occurring valuable or useful substance such as wood, fruit, or medicinal plants*

KEY

1. **forest floor**—a dark and gloomy layer (receiving only 1–2 percent of sunlight), with a carpet of dead leaves

2. **Goliath tarantula**—the largest spider in the world; feeds on frogs, lizards, mice, and small snakes

3. **jaguar**—a large hunter that silently stalks wild pigs, rats, deer, and armadillos along rainforest trails

4. **understory**—a shady layer with insects, a tangle of vines, and small trees and animals

5. **leaf-cutter ants**—carry leaf pieces to nests under the ground to make compost to grow fungus for food

6. **emerald tree boa**—camouflaged among the green leaves, this snake snatches prey in its sharp teeth

7. **drip tip**—this long point on a leaf helps rainwater drip away, stopping harmful algae from growing

8. **epiphyte**—a plant, such as this bromeliad, that perches on the branches of trees to get closer to the light

9. **red howler monkey**—calls out to warn other howlers to stay off its patch; it's hard to see through the thick forest, so sound is useful for communication

OTHER FORESTS

The two main types of cooler forests are the deciduous and coniferous forests in northern regions. They are dominated by the changing seasons. In the winter, animals migrate to warmer places farther south or hide in burrows. A few animals hibernate, or sleep through the winter.

Coniferous trees have needle-shaped leaves to help snow slide off in the winter. The trees produce seeds in cones.

Deciduous trees, unlike coniferous ones, have wide, flat leaves that change color and drop off in the fall.

> The tallest tree in the world, a giant sequoia, is more than 367 ft. (112m) tall—the height of a 37-story building!

TUNDRA—cold, windy, treeless area found on the edges of the Arctic and Antarctica

Penguins at the South Pole

Penguins and polar bears never meet because penguins live only in and around Antarctica, while polar bears live in northern Arctic lands. Penguins spend most of their lives at sea, using their stiff flippers to "fly" underwater. Their dense, waterproof feathers and thick layers of fatty blubber keep the birds warm. Penguins come onto land or sea ice in order to breed, often forming huge colonies of up to a million birds.

short, stubby tail used as a prop to help penguin stand up and as a rudder for steering underwater

colony of Emperor penguins in Antarctica

POLAR LANDS

The coldest places on the planet are at the top and bottom of the world—the Arctic is a frozen ocean around the North Pole, and Antarctica is a frozen continent around the South Pole. They both have bitterly cold winters and short, warm summers, when the sun never sets. The poles are ringed by areas of tundra. Many animals visit polar lands in the summer to feed and raise their young, but only a few very hardy animals, such as polar bears, can survive in polar lands all year long.

Summer vacation

Huge herds of reindeer, or caribou, are summer visitors to the flat, treeless tundra lands around the Arctic. They spend the winter feeding and sheltering in conifer forests farther south. In the summer, they migrate, walking thousands of miles to the tundra, where there is food and few predators.

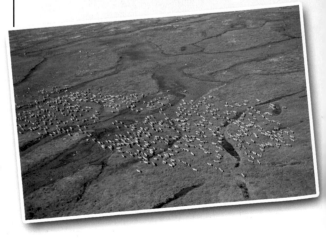

> Most polar fish have a natural chemical "antifreeze" in their blood, which keeps them from freezing solid in icy water.

The chicks huddle together for warmth during snow blizzards. Their parents make long journeys to and from the sea to collect fish for them. They recognize their chicks by their high-pitched calls.

⊖ CAMOUFLAGE

The thick fur coat of the Arctic fox changes color to hide the animal in its habitat as it hunts for prey such as birds and voles. This is called camouflage. In the winter, when the ground is snowy and icy, the fox grows thick white fur. In the summer, the white fur is replaced by a thinner coat of brownish-gray fur. This camouflages the fox against the brown and gray rocks and soil that appear as the snow and ice melt.

Arctic fox in the summer

Arctic fox in the winter

Polar plants

No plants grow at the snowy poles, but some tough plants live on the bleak tundra, where the snow and ice melts during the summer. Simple plants, such as mosses and lichens, survive the intense cold, thin, frozen soil and short growing season. They grow in low "cushions" to stay out of the wind and trap moisture.

The cubs stay with their mother for one or two years. They wrestle with each other to practice hunting skills, and they watch their mother catching the seals that swim beneath the sea ice so that they can learn how to catch food on their own.

The ice bear

In the middle of the Arctic winter, a mother polar bear gives birth to two tiny cubs inside a snow den. For six months, she stays hidden away while her cubs drink her rich milk. She cannot leave the den to eat until the cubs are strong enough to go outside. She survives by using the energy stored in her thick body fat, which also keeps her warm.

EARTH'S RESOURCES

From fuels and metals to gems and construction materials, people take all kinds of natural resources from planet Earth. Some of these resources, such as water and sand, are renewable, while others, such as oil and gas, are nonrenewable and will run out one day. Natural resources can be dug up near Earth's surface, but many are extracted from deep under the ground or even under the ocean.

Ocean skyscraper

More than 557 ft. (170m) taller than the Eiffel Tower, this huge platform was built to extract gas from beneath the seabed. Its "legs" reach 985 ft. (300m) under the ocean's surface, and its "feet" are embedded in the sea floor. Pipes tap into reservoirs (large pockets) of gas, which lie trapped beneath thick layers of rock. Gas, like coal and oil, is a fossil fuel—it is made from the fossilized remains of plants and animals.

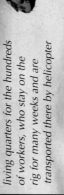

living quarters for the hundreds of workers, who stay on the rig for many weeks and are transported there by helicopter

helicopter landing platform

From plants to coal

Most coal was formed from plants that grew in swamps about 300 million years ago. The decaying plants were buried in mud, where heat and pressure turned them into coal. Coal often forms in horizontal seams. Shafts are sunk from the surface and tunnels dug along the seams.

This gas rig in the North Sea is 1,548 ft. (472m) high (including its underwater section) and weighs almost one million tons. Like all platforms, it generates its own electricity and converts salt water into fresh water.

> FUEL—a material, such as coal, oil, gas, or wood, that provides energy, usually by burning

● BUILDING BLOCKS

Most building materials can be dug up. We use clay (thick mud) to make bricks and roof tiles, stones for walls and sidewalks, sand to make glass, and gravel to build roads. Cement, used for "gluing" together bricks, is made by heating crushed limestone and clay and mixing this with sand and water. Sand and gravel are added to cement to form concrete.

Bricks can be made from clay, mixed with water and straw, and dried solid in molds in the sun.

walls of steel-reinforced concrete more than 3.3 ft (1m) thick can withstand the huge pressure of water

The pockets of gas, accessed by pipes, lie up to 0.6 mi. (1km) beneath the seabed.

KEY

1 platform supply ship—delivers goods that are too heavy to transport by helicopter; a cable links an underwater robot to the ship

2 underwater robot, or ROV (remotely operated vehicle)—inspects the platform for damage and carries out research and repairs

3 reinforced concrete box—connects the legs, helping lessen the vibrations caused by waves hitting the platform

4 pipes inside legs—carry gas up to the platform for filtering, then convey gas back down the legs again before exporting to the mainland

5 pipes along seabed—transport gas, at speeds of up to 1,860 mph (3,000km/h), to a processing plant on land or to another platform

> Scientists estimate that oil reserves will last about 50 years, natural gas reserves about 70 years, and coal reserves about 150–250 years.

CHANGING CLIMATE

The planet's climate has been changing naturally for millions of years because of changes to Earth's path around the Sun and events such as volcanic eruptions. In the age of dinosaurs, the world was warmer and there were no polar icecaps. But only 18,000 years ago, ice sheets covered large parts of North America and Europe. Now, the climate is warming up unnaturally fast because of the pollution that people are pumping into the atmosphere.

Melting ice

Warmer global temperatures are causing sea ice and glaciers to melt rapidly. The extra water flowing into the sea is making sea levels rise. Water expands when it is heated, making sea levels rise even faster.

A warmer planet

Gases in the planet's atmosphere, especially carbon dioxide (CO_2), trap heat on Earth, stopping it from escaping into space. These gases work like the glass in a greenhouse to warm up the planet. Vehicles, factories, and burning forests are releasing more and more "greenhouse gases" into the atmosphere, contributing to global warming. By the end of the 2000s, Earth is likely to have heated up by 4–9°F (2–5°C). This small rise will have serious consequences.

Earth releases some heat into space.

Trees absorb carbon dioxide to make their food but release the carbon dioxide stored in their bodies when forests are burned.

Sunlight heats Earth's surface.

Pollution from vehicles, factories, airplanes, and ships sends greenhouse gases into the atmosphere.

Greenhouse gases in the atmosphere trap some heat given off by Earth.

Cutting down forests reduces the amount of carbon dioxide taken out of the atmosphere by plants.

> Today, the average global temperature is about 9°F (5°C) higher than during the last glacial period.

The Viedma Glacier, Argentina, could disappear within 60 years. As ice reflects the Sun's heat back into space, less ice on the planet means that less heat is reflected away from Earth.

Rising sea levels

Sea levels may rise by 4 in. (10cm) to 3.3 ft. (1m) by 2100. This will flood small, low islands, countries such as Bangladesh and the Netherlands, and threaten cities such as New York; London, England; and Shanghai, China.

Low-lying islands could disappear under the waves.

Extreme weather

Hurricanes, tornadoes, blizzards, and other storms may become more common as our planet heats up. Warmer air can hold more water, causing heavy rainfall and floods in many areas. But in places such as Australia and Africa there will be droughts.

satellite image showing three positions of Hurricane Andrew as it hits the Caribbean islands and the United States

"What changed in the U.S. with Hurricane Katrina was the feeling that we have entered a period of consequences."

Al Gore (born 1948)
Environmental activist and former U.S. vice president

Changing ecosystems

Life has evolved over millions of years to cope with changing climates. Some species have died out, but new ones have developed to take their places. However, if the climate changes too quickly, some wildlife will die out. Up to 30–40 percent of all species could be extinct by the year 2050.

Coral reefs, one of the planet's richest ecosystems, die when the ocean becomes too hot.

Forest fires

Higher temperatures dry out vegetation, increasing the risk of forest fires, especially at the end of long, hot summers. As Earth heats up, fires could occur over larger areas and happen more often. This will release the carbon dioxide locked up in trees into the atmosphere, causing the planet to warm up even more quickly.

Farming problems

Global warming will affect the types of crops grown in different parts of the world. Crops such as corn and sugar cane do not grow well in high temperatures. Droughts in Africa, Southeast Asia, and China will turn farmland into desert, and many people could suffer from famine.

www.epa.gov/climatechange/kids

LOOKING AFTER EARTH

Earth's population is likely to rise to almost nine billion by 2050. Such an immense number of people will drain natural resources, pollute the land, sea, and skies, and change habitats and climate, making life impossible for many plants and animals. We need to take much better care of our planet now—everyone can help do this, including you!

A dripping faucet can waste 2,400 gal. (9,000 liters) of water a year! To save water: take showers, not baths; turn off the faucet while brushing your teeth; and put a brick in a plastic bag in the toilet tank to reduce the amount of water used per flush.

Cars of the future

Dangerous emissions from cars have greatly added to climate change. Hybrid cars have an electric battery as well as a gasoline engine. The battery produces no emissions at all, but if recharging it uses electricity from a fossil-fuel power plant, the car still pollutes the environment. It is not a "zero emission" form of transportation, such as cycling.

Air flows easily over the "streamlined" car, reducing "drag" that would slow it down. This means the car can travel farther before its battery runs out.

Chevrolet's Volt hybrid car

The battery takes three to eight hours to charge, costing about 75 cents. This will power the car for 40 mi. (60km). Charging the car daily uses less electricity per year than a refrigerator.

The wheels are never directly driven by the engine. If the battery runs out, the engine powers an electric drive unit that produces more electricity.

Making recycled paper uses only half the energy and less than one-third of the water needed to make paper from trees.

Save energy

Within the next 100 years, coal, oil, and gas, which cause pollution when they are used for fuel, will be too expensive for everyday use. We need to generate energy from nonpolluting renewable sources such as wind, water, the Sun, or hot rocks underground. We also need to use less energy by not leaving the TV on standby; putting on a sweater instead of turning up the heat; using energy-saving light bulbs; and turning off lights and air conditioners when not needed.

http://footprint.wwf.org.uk

These wind turbines generate enough electricity to supply thousands of homes without polluting the environment.

An employee of a recycling company in Germany surveys a mountain of glass bottles and jars. Recycling just one glass bottle saves enough energy to power a computer for 25 minutes.

Reuse and recycle

Every month, each of us throws away our own body weight in trash. Much of that waste can be reused or recycled. We can recycle all sorts of materials, from cans, cell phones, and paper to plastics, ink cartridges, and leftover food. Recycling saves resources, money, energy, and habitats and reduces pollution.

Take a carbon diet

Reduce the amount of carbon dioxide you send into the atmosphere each year. Start by calculating your carbon footprint using the website listed in the panel above right.

amount of carbon dioxide produced per year by a U.S. resident

22.4 tons

⊖ REDUCE PACKAGING

A large amount of packaging is not really necessary. About 20 percent of household waste is made up of packaging, and about 16 percent of the cost of a product pays for the packaging! Try to buy items with less packaging, and use your own shopping bags instead of new plastic ones. Refills and family-size packages will also help you reduce your waste.

Try to buy loose fruit and vegetables rather than those packaged with plastic wrap, trays, or boxes.

GLOSSARY

atmosphere
A blanket of gases around a planet, moon, or star that is held there by the force of gravity.

axis
An imaginary line that passes through the poles of a planet and on which the planet spins.

climate
The average pattern of weather in a place over a long period.

comet
A ball of frozen gas and dust that travels around (orbits) the Sun. Some of the gas and dust streams out from the comet to make a "tail."

coniferous
Relating to plants that reproduce by making seeds in cones. Most coniferous plants are evergreen trees or shrubs.

continent
One of the seven large areas of land on Earth, including Africa, Antarctica, Asia, Australia, Europe, North America, and South America.

crust
The thin, rocky outer layer of planet Earth. There are two different types of crust: thicker, lightweight continental crust and the thinner, heavier oceanic crust found under the oceans.

deciduous
Relating to trees that lose their leaves at the end of the growing season each fall. *Deciduous* means "falling off."

density
The mass of a substance per unit of volume.

element
A substance that cannot be broken down into simpler substances by chemical reactions.

equator
An imaginary line around the middle of Earth, halfway between the North Pole and the South Pole.

erosion
The removal of soil and pieces of rock on Earth's surface by wind, water, or ice.

fault
A crack in Earth's crust where blocks of rock slip past each other. Faults happen as a result of plate movements or stresses within the rocks.

fossil
The remains or traces of prehistoric living things preserved in rocks. Most fossils are found in sedimentary rocks that are exposed on the surface of Earth.

glacial period
A long period with a very cold climate, when ice sheets cover large areas of Earth. An ice age is a period in which any amount of ice is present at the poles.

global warming
A general warming of Earth's atmosphere caused by pollution from greenhouse gases (especially carbon dioxide).

gravity
An invisible force that pulls every object in the universe (everything that exists) toward every other object. Big objects, such as planets, have the strongest gravity. It is gravity that pulls down everything on Earth to the ground and that gives things weight.

habitat

The physical surroundings in which an animal or plant lives, including the climate and features of the landscape.

hemisphere

One-half of a sphere. The equator divides Earth into northern and southern hemispheres.

hybrid car

A car that uses two or more sources of energy (such as gasoline, diesel, electricity, or hydrogen) to power it.

magma

Very hot molten (melted) rock from beneath Earth's surface. When magma spills onto the surface, it is called lava.

magnetic field

The magnetic force that surrounds Earth because of the planet's dense iron core, which acts like a giant magnet.

mantle

The thick, rocky middle layer of the planet between the crust and the core. Its rocks transfer heat from the middle of Earth to its surface.

meteor

A trail of light in the sky caused by a piece of rock or metal falling from space and burning up in our atmosphere. If part of the object reaches Earth's surface, it is called a meteorite.

mineral

A natural substance from Earth's crust that has a definite chemical composition and a particular crystal structure and does not come from animals or plants. Minerals are the building blocks of rocks.

natural resource

A naturally occurring valuable or useful substance such as wood, clay, or oil.

ozone

A form of oxygen gas that forms a thin layer in the atmosphere, about 12 mi. (20km) above Earth. The ozone layer filters out harmful ultraviolet radiation from the Sun.

radiation

A form of energy that travels through space as electromagnetic waves. Different types of radiation include light, x-rays, and ultraviolet radiation.

renewable

Relating to something that can be used over and over again without running out. The wind, waves, and the Sun's heat are forms of renewable, or "alternative," energy.

sediment

Small, solid pieces of rock debris, such as sand or mud, moved away from their place of origin by wind, water, or ice.

temperate climate

A mild, rainy climate that is neither too hot nor too cold. Places with a temperate climate are found between the hot tropical regions and the cold poles.

tide

The regular rise and fall of the water in the oceans owing to the pull of gravity from the Moon and the Sun.

tropical climate

A hot climate with periods of heavy rainfall. Places near the equator have a tropical climate.

weathering

The gradual breaking down of rocks by the weather, chemicals, or plants.

INDEX

INVESTIGATE

A satellite orbits Earth, taking pictures of it.

Find out more about Earth, its place in the solar system, and how it is changing by checking out websites, books, and museums.

Earth in space

You don't have to be an astronaut to explore our planet from space. Look up satellite photographs of Earth in books or on the Internet or visit space centers and museums.

Navigators Stars & Planets by Dr. Mike Goldsmith (Kingfisher)

U.S. Space & Rocket Center, One Tranquility Base, Huntsville, AL 35805

www.earthfromspace.si.edu/online_exhibition.asp

BedZED, the United Kingdom's largest ecovillage.

Looking after our planet

Understand more about how Earth functions and find out how you can help it survive.

Kingfisher Knowledge Endangered Planet by David Burnie (Kingfisher)

Museum of the Earth, 1259 Trumansburg Road, Ithaca, NY 14850

www.worldwildlife.org

Always go hiking with a group and stick to well-marked trails.

Exploring the great outdoors

Go outside and explore your planet! Borrow some binoculars and go for a walk in the woods or a park. What plants can you see, and what wildlife can you spot?

Wildlife of North America: A Naturalist's Lifelist by Whit Bronaugh (University Press of Florida)

Yellowstone National Park, P.O. Box 168, Yellowstone National Park, WY 82190-0168

www.nps.gov/learn/parkfun.htm

fossil hunting on a stony beach

Rocks and fossils

Take a closer look at the rocks beneath your feet and the fossils that tell the history of life on our planet. Go on a guided tour of mines or caves deep underground.

Basher Science: Rocks and Minerals by Dan Green and Simon Basher (Kingfisher)

Atlas Coal Mine National Historic Site, Box 521, 110 Century Drive, East Coulee, Alberta, Canada T0J 1B0

www.mineraltown.com